EDITOR: LEE JOH

OSPREY MILITARY MEN-AT-ARMS SERIES

MUGHUL INDIA
1504-1761

Text by
DAVID NICOLLE PhD
Colour plates by
ANGUS McBRIDE

First published in Great Britain in 1993
by Osprey, an imprint of Reed Consumer Books Limited
Michelin House, 81 Fulham Road
London SW3 6RB
and Auckland, Melbourne, Singapore and Toronto

ISBN 1 85532 3443

Filmset in Great Britain
Printed through Bookbuilders Ltd, Hong Kong

Dedication
A little one for Katie,
'cause they're pretty like her.

Artist's Note
Readers may care to note that the original paintings
from which the colour plates in this book were
prepared are available for private sale. All
reproduction copyright whatsoever is retained by the
publisher. All enquiries should be addressed to:
  Scorpio
  PO Box 475,
  Hailsham,
  E. Sussex BN27 2SL
The publishers regret that they can enter into no
correspondence upon this matter.

Publisher's Note
Readers may wish to study this title in conjunction
with the following Osprey publications:
MAA 105 *The Mongols*
MAA 222 *The Age of Tamerlane*
MAA 140 *The Ottoman Turks*
MAA 259 *The Mamluks 1250–1517*

For a catalogue of all books published by Osprey Military
please write to:

**The Marketing Manager,
Consumer Catalogue Department,
Osprey Publishing Ltd,
Michelin House, 81 Fulham Road,
London SW3 6RB**

INTRODUCTION

The name Mughul is often spelt 'Mughal' or 'Mogul', in English, where it also has the modern secondary meaning of 'tycoon'. Here we use the more accurate transliteration of the word which is, in fact, merely the Arabic-Persian name for a Mongol. Babur, the founder of the Mughul dynasty, was of Turco-Mongol origin – he was descended from Timur-i-Lenk (Tamerlane) on his father's side and Genghiz Khan on his mother's[1]. Though Babur disliked being called a Mongol and much preferred to be known as a Turk, the name 'Mughul' stuck; and succeeding rulers of the dynasty became known in Europe as the Great Moguls.

Mughul India has not always been treated kindly by historians. During the British domination of India the Mughul period was often portrayed as a barbarous age which inevitably gave way to European rule. Some modern Indian historians have also criticised the Mughuls for failing to save India from British conquest. The Mughuls were also, of course, foreign conquerors, and represented a Muslim minority which dominated Hindu India for centuries.

In fact, much of India had been under Muslim rule long before Babur invaded the sub-continent and set up the Mughul state. The small pre-Mughul Muslim population included indigenous Indians who had converted for economic or political reasons as well as religious ones. They were ruled by an élite that claimed descent from various conquerors, including Arab families which had lived in north-west India for almost a thousand years. In northern and central India, however, most of the local military aristocracy claimed Persian, Afghan, Turkish or Mongol ancestry. The pre-Mughul Muslim states also had close links with other Muslim states, not only with neighbouring Afghanistan and Transoxania but with western Iran, Iraq, and even eastern Turkey.

Pre-Mughul Muslim armies in India were similar to those of other eastern Muslim states and owed relatively little to native Indian military tradition. The entire Muslim minority seems to have had military obligations – a concept rooted in the earliest days of Islam – and public military displays were popular, particularly in the Holy Month of Muharram. Another characteristic of these Muslim armies was their multi-ethnic character. By the 15th century the armies of the ruling Turco-Muslim dynasties were essentially 'feudal' in the sense that the military élite lived off land granted by the Sultan. On the other hand such land-grants were already being bought and sold by non-military middle-men (for a more detailed description of 14th–15th century Muslim military 'feudalism' see MAA 259 *The Mamluks 1250–1517*).

The armies of pre-Mughul northern India were also equipped in much the same way as those of neighbouring Muslim states, Timurid influence being particularly strong in the 15th century. By the early 16th century Ottoman Turkish influence was apparent in the armies of Gujarat – a coastal region having particularly strong trading links with the Middle East – and firearms were already in use.

The situation in southern India was different, for here Muslim conquest took place relatively late. The indigenous Hindu population had been strictly divided into military and non-military castes, but conversion to Islam now opened up military career opportunities to everyone. Even so the Muslim states of the Deccan had only a small ruling Muslim élite, who made considerable use of their Hindu subjects' martial skills.

The Mughul State

At the end of the 15th century, Babur and his followers came out of Transoxania, where the last of the Timurid dynasty had been defending the settled

---

[1] See MAA 222 *The Age of Tamerlane* and MAA 105 *The Mongols.*

agricultural zone against yet another nomad invasion, this time by the Uzbeks (see MAA 222 *The Age of Tamerlane*). Babur was a member of a cultured Timurid élite which, though of Turco-Mongol origin, was strongly influenced by the military traditions of Iran.

First, Babur carved out a state in Afghanistan, effectively as a continuation of Timurid rule; from there he went on to gradually conquer north-western India. In the Timurid mind, however, the empire belonged to a ruling family, not to a single ruler. Each new ruler emerged from many contenders, being selected for piety, valour,

generosity and military power. Not until the reign of the third Mughul ruler, Akbar, was power concentrated in the hands of the ruler himself. Akbar and his successors then had to struggle to maintain royal authority in the face of the basically democratic spirit of Islam. Mughul rulers also adopted many aspects of Hindu kingship, with an extraordinary ritualisation of court life. Mughul royal display, costume and splendour not only dazzled visiting Europeans but even amazed the rulers of neighbouring Iran and the Ottoman Empire – who were hardly paupers themselves.

The extent to which the Mughuls really dominated the outlying provinces of their vast empire is questionable, but they certainly tried to control the main communications and economic centres, while also encouraging agriculture, trade, art and science. Paradoxically the aboriginal peoples of India fared better at the hands of these alien Mughuls than at the hands of local Hindu rulers. The Mughuls certainly enslaved many Dravidian and Kolarian forest tribesmen, but the Hindu Marathas simply massacred them. At first the Mughul army was based upon Timurid traditions which were themselves closer to the Mongol than strictly Islamic military ideas. Once the Mughul state was established in India, however, Muslim and Hindu military traditions soon had a powerful impact. The army became essentially mercenary, consisting of paid professional volunteers.

The decline of the Mughul state really started when Jahangir rebelled against his father Akbar. Jahangir's own son Khusru subsequently rebelled against him. The Muslim-Sikh hatred which persists to this day also started in Jahangir's reign. The next Mughul ruler, Shah-jahan, reigned during a time of extraordinary magnificence which masked the problems of the Mughul empire. Under his successor Aurangzib, northern and western Afghanistan broke away; these regions were simply too far from Delhi to get proper military support. Within five years of Aurangzib's death the empire collapsed into civil war, rebellion and fragmentation. Nevertheless the Mughuls' prestige long outlasted their exercise of effective power.

After a brief Persian invasion early in the 18th century Mughul Delhi was squabbled over by Afghans from the west and Hindu Marathas from

The Growth of the Mughul Empire

- Babur's conquests c.1530
- under Akbar c.1600
- under Aurangzib c.1690
- ◇ European trading settlements late 17 century

the south. Various rebel movements drew strength from the Hindu peasantry's deep resentment of the Indo-Muslim military aristocracy. The followers of a new religion, the Sikhs, were also challenging Muslim military domination. By this time there had been a revival of Hindu military power, most obviously in the shape of the Marathas of the Deccan. The last and least likely of groups to be squabbling over the decaying Mughul Empire were foreign merchant companies, each supported by its own private army. Between 1765 and 1771 Shah Alam II placed what was left of the Mughul empire under British protection; but that, as they say, is another story.

CHRONOLOGY

1482 Birth of Babur in Farghana, Transoxania, in Central Asia.
1494 Babur becomes ruler of Farghana.
1501 Babur loses Samarkand.
1504 Babur occupies Kabul.
1509 Albuquerque becomes governor of Portuguese possessions in India.

1526 Babur defeats Sultan Ibrahim Lodi of northern India at first battle of Panipat, and occupies Delhi as first Mughul ruler of northern India.
1530 Death of Babur; Humayun becomes Mughul ruler.
1540 Humayun defeated near Kanauj, followed by loss of almost all northern India to Shir Khan.
1555 Humayun retakes Delhi.
1556 Death of Humayun; Akbar becomes Mughul Emperor and defeats Indians at second battle of Panipat.
1558–1601 Akbar conquers almost all of northern India and Afghanistan.
1605 Death of Akbar; Jahangir becomes Mughul Emperor.
1611 English establish first commercial base at Masulipatam.
1622–24 Shah-jahan rebels against his father, the Emperor Jahangir, in Afghanistan.
1627 Death of Jahangir.
1628 Shah-jahan becomes Mughul Emperor.
1632 Mughul invasion of the Deccan.
1646 Shivaji, leader of the Marathas, captures Torna; the start of the rise of the Marathas.

Cavalry and infantry in combat in a manuscript of Nizami's Khamseh made at Herat c.1493. The arms and armour used would be the same as that of Babur's first armies, including those which invaded India. (British Library, Ms. 25900, f.231v)

1649 Persians invade Mughul-ruled Afghanistan.

1656–7 Mughul invasion of Hyderabad.

1657–9 Mughul civil war of succession.

1659 Imprisonment of Shah-jahan (dies in 1666); Aurangzib becomes Mughul Emperor.

1661 Bombay ceded to the English.

1669 Jats rebel against Mughul rule.

1675 Execution of Teg Bahadur, spiritual leader of new Sikh religion.

1681 Mughuls lose control of Kamarupa; Aurangzib invades Deccan.

1686–90 English war against Mughuls.

1687 Mughuls seize Golkonda in the Deccan.

1699–1706 Major Maratha raids across southern India.

1707 Death of Aurangzib; Bahadur Shah becomes Mughul Emperor.

1712 Death of Bahadur Shah; Jahandar Shah becomes Mughul Emperor.

1713 Murder of Jahandar Shah; Farrukhsiyar becomes Mughul Emperor.

1719 Farrukhsiyar executed.

1719–20 Rivalry of four unsuccessful pretenders to Mughul throne; Muhammad Shah becomes Mughul Emperor.

1724 Nizam (governor) of Hyderabad virtually independent in the Deccan.

1725 Shuja al Din effectively independent as Governor of Bengal.

1735 Mughuls recognise Maratha rule over central India.

1739 Persians capture Delhi and hold it briefly.

1739–42 Maratha invasions of northern India.

1744–48 First Anglo-French war in India.

1747 Afghanistan independent under Ahmad Khan Durrani; gradually conquers north-western India.

1748 Death of Muhammad Shah; Ahmad Shah becomes Mughul Emperor.

1754 Death of Ahmad; 'Alamgir II becomes Mughul Emperor.

1756–63 Seven Years War (Britain & Prussia v. France, Austria & Russia) also involves British & French forces in India.

1757 English under Robert Clive defeat French at battle of Plassey.

1759 Death of 'Alamgir II; Shah 'Alam becomes Mughul Emperor.

1761 Afghans defeat Marathas at third battle of Panipat; Mughuls rule only the area around Delhi as Maratha puppets.

THE FIRST MUGHULS

Babur, the first Mughul ruler of India, was a member of the Turkish ruling élite of Transoxania, a part of the state set up by Tamerlane in the 14th century. Babur was thrown into small-scale warfare for the control of various towns as the Timurid state collapsed before the advancing Uzbeks. After gaining and then losing the great city of Samarkand, Babur decided, in 1504, to seek his fortune to the south; he won Kabul two years later.

'Ghengiz Khan's army attacks a fortress', in the Ghengiz Khan Nama made for the Mughul Emperor Akbar c.1596. Though purporting to show 13th-century events, the Mongols in this illustration are actually 16th-century Mughul troops, including unarmoured Hindu infantry, a gunner priming his cannon, Mughul matchlock men, and archers shooting from behind large wooden mantlets. (National Library, Tehran)

For some years Babur operated as a client of the powerful Safavid rulers of Iran, but finally gave up his northern dreams in 1512; he began looking instead to the south-east. His first raid into India in 1516 was followed by several others, and by the time of his death in 1530 Babur's troops had reached Bengal on the far side of the sub-continent.

To modern eyes Babur seems an aggressive figure waging war on all and sundry, but he had much in common with the *condottieri* military leaders of Renaissance Italy. With no particular national loyalties, he fought mainly for the benefit of his family. During his own lifetime, though, he was seen as an attractive figure: resilient, brave, cheerful, a skilled poet and a successful if cautious general.

Babur's first armies were small and consisted of Turkish, Mongol, Iranian and Afghan troops. Most of the Turks were known as *yigit*, 'braves' in Turkish, their officers being called *begs*. The Turkish military élite were cultivated men: when too old to serve as soldiers many of them took up painting, poetry or the making of high-quality bows. Babur's immediate entourage was his *khasa tabin* consisting of the best soldiers divided into units of ten and 50 under trained officers. In general, however, Babur's cavalry seems to have been organised in large *tuman*, units led by *tumandar* officers, a structure little changed since the time of the original Mongol armies of Genghiz Khan.

The main strength of Babur's army lay in its superior discipline and tactics, areas in which Babur learned much from his first Uzbek foes. Babur could reinforce such discipline with ferocious punishments, though these were rarely used in practice, and then usually only to set an example. Babur's own remarkably detailed autobiography, the *Babur Nama* (literally 'The Book of Babur'), also provides interesting details about the equipment of those first Mughul armies. Élite cavalry used horse-armour. Guns were already known, and some matchlock muskets were already powerful enough to shoot right through existing shields and cuirasses.

This was a time of change, not only with the introduction of firearms but also in tactics, although traditional Turkish ways of fighting remained important. For example, in 1507 Babur's cavalry seized control of the steep slopes of a mountain

'*Kublai Khan's army pursues the Chinese across the river Yang Tse Kiang*', in the Ghengiz Khan Nama *made for the Mughul Emperor Akbar c.1596. Again this manuscript* anachronistically depicts typical 16th-century Mughul heavy cavalry using sabres and maces and riding armoured horses. (National Library, Tehran)

valley so that they could pour volleys of arrows on their foes below. Outside Samarkand a cavalry army dismounted so that it could shoot more accurately, but was then caught by a sudden enemy charge before it could remount. Babur seems to have combined traditional tactics with the latest ideas. Some victories he won by first sending horse-archers to harass the foe in the ancient manner, to be followed by infantry matchlock gunners supported by horse-archers on each flank. The *Babur Nama* also records the shooting of messages attached to arrows into an enemy camp; and that during a particularly long siege the garrison's valuable horses could be fed on mulberry or elm

AKBAR'S REFORMS

Miniature from the Anwar-i Sulayh, a Mughul manuscript made around 1570, showing a man riding a two-humped Bactrian camel. He is armed with a curved sabre and a typical Indian jamdhar thrusting dagger. (SOAS, London)

Humayun's son Akbar was probably the greatest Mughul ruler. He tolerated all religions and even tried to unite his Muslim and Hindu subjects with a new religion of his own called the *Din Ilahi* or 'Divine Faith'. Akbar also restructured the Mughul state and army. He wanted his army to be a standing force of full-time professionals paid directly from the treasury. The land was to be divided into new units supporting a new military structure. Above all Akbar wanted to regularise officer ranks. Everyone, he intended, would enter at the lowest grade and would rise by merit alone. But Akbar's reforms were at first very unpopular and only seem to have been imposed in the central areas of the empire. Nor did the new military structure always work properly. During a Mughul invasion of the Deccan in 1599, for example, the army almost mutinied because pay was not getting through and the men were going hungry.

Officer ranks (*mansabs*)

A great deal is known about Akbar's new army structure, the basis of which were 33 *mansabs* or officer ranks. All *mansabdars* or rank-holders were appointed in theory by the ruler. The three most senior – *mansabdars* of 10,000, 8,000 and 7,000 – were reserved for princes. The rest went from *mansabdar* of 5,000 to *mansabdar* of 10. In this highly complex system only *mansabdars* of a certain status could serve in contingents commanded by the most senior *mansabdars*; lower ranking *mansabdars* were not allowed to do so. Each rank was also expected to maintain a certain number of horses and other animals: a *mansabdar* of 5,000, for example, was to possess 340 horses of specified types, 90 elephants, 80 camels, 20 mules and 160 carts. At the other end of the scale a *mansabdar* of 10 was to have four horses but no other animals.

To confuse the issue further, a second number was later attached to each rank to give an indication of actual military obligations: so a man might be known as a *mansabdar* 4,000/2,000 or a *mansabdar* 3,000/3,000. The first figure was his *zat* or original

tree leaves or, if desperate, on dampened wood shavings.

It was with such a basically Turkish Central Asian army that Babur invaded India. The backlash came during the reign of his son, Humayun, who was at one time driven into Afghanistan. During the wars of Humayun's reign the Mughul army evolved further, keeping the best Central Asian traditions while learning from its Indian enemies. Gujarat on the coast of the Arabian Sea had, for example, already received advanced military assistance, first from the Mamluks of Egypt and then from the Ottoman Turks in their struggle against Portuguese piracy. The army of Humayun's most dedicated foe, Shir Khan, was particularly efficient. It was famous for the careful way in which all cavalry horses were branded according to rank and ownership. Shir Khan's successors, who resisted the Mughuls until 1554, reorganised this force into cavalry units of 50, 200, 250, and 500 troopers, a system which may have provided the model for Akbar's military reforms in the later 16th century.

military status, the second or *sawar* figure indicated true obligations. There were also *mashrut sawar* or 'acting ranks', held by men who had to carry out duties above their ranks, probably as temporary measures.

During Akbar's reign all *mansabdars* of 500 and above could be called *mirs*, from the Arabic *amir*, though by the time of Shah-jahan only *mansabdars* of 1,000 and above were given this title. Some *mirs* had specific duties, such as the *Mir Bakhshi*, who acted like a quartermaster-general in charge of army transport and paying the troops while on active service. (In peacetime the army pay was handled by the *diwan*, a government department under the *Wazir* or Prime Minister.) Another important senior *mir* was the *Mir Saman*, who was in charge of all military workshops, arsenals and stores.

It was considered very important for each unit to have an opportunity to serve close to the ruler and to get the financial rewards associated with service at court. Akbar introduced a complex rotation system to make this possible: the army was divided into 12 parts, each of which came to court for a year's duty. The army was also divided into 12 other sections, each of which was responsible for mounting guard for one month every year. At yet another level, the four main divisions of the army were subdivided into seven smaller sections, each responsible for *chauki* or mounting guard at the palace one day a week. Senior noblemen had to attend court even more frequently, and when the emperor was with the army they had to appear at his headquarters every morning and evening.

One of the most fundamental changes that Akbar introduced concerned military pay. Theoretically all *mansabdars* would get their money directly from central treasuries. In reality the system grew increasingly complex with many factors affecting just what each man received. Under Akbar himself the top-grade *mansabdar* of 5,000 got 30,000 rupees a month, with correspondingly less for the lower ranks. *Jagirs* or estates were given to senior *mansabdars* to support them and their followers, but, like the *iqta* military estates of earlier Muslim centuries, these could not be inherited. The salary of a *tabinan* or ordinary cavalry trooper was based on the types of horses he had to maintain. The *tabinan's* officer also deducted five per cent from the man's salary to cover administrative and equipment costs. All ranks, including *mansabdars*, could get salary increments, additional *jagirs* or cash prizes for good conduct.

The Mughul system of military promotion was well defined if somewhat bureaucratic, particularly when it came to the selection of *mansabdar* officers. A man would first present a *haqiqat* or application. If this was accepted he would make obeisance at court. His *haqiqat* would then be kept in the *bakhshi's* office while the man was given a *tasdiq* or certificate of rank. Next he would have to go to a

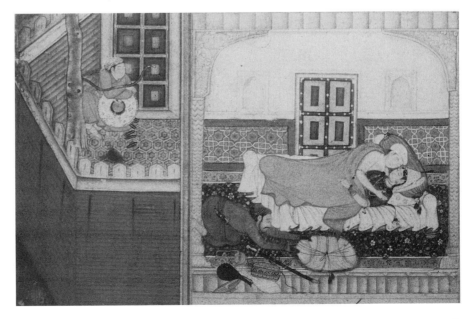

In this humorous illumination from the Anwar-i Sulah *made around 1570, a thief with a straight sword robs a man as he sleeps. A guard is also asleep outside, his bow slung around his neck. (SOAS, London)*

series of offices getting signatures until the *tasdiq* was complete.

Though there was no real regimental structure in the Mughul army, some larger formations do seem to have been subdivided. The fundamental unit was, however, the *mansabdar* with his own followers. The size of such units varied according to the *mansabdar's* status, but each appears to have included *tabinan* troopers of 'one horse', 'two horse' and 'three horse' ranks.

The Mughul army also included many provincial and auxiliary forces. The Empire itself consisted of large *suba* provinces sub-divided into many small *sarkar* districts, where local defence and good order were the responsibility of a *Faujdar*, supposedly appointed directly by the Emperor's government in Delhi. Each *sarkar* consisted of smaller *pargana* or *mahal* tax units. Separate from this local administration were various auxiliary forces called *kumaki*, who were recruited from a great variety of sources.

As with nearly all pre-modern armies, it is impossible to be certain about the size of Mughul forces; but reasonably good estimates can be made. It is fairly clear that Babur's army in Afghanistan in 1507 numbered no more than 2,000 men. By the time of Babur's fifth invasion of India it might have grown to 15,000 or even 20,000. Once the Mughuls were firmly established in India the numbers increased dramatically: by the late 17th century Aurangzib may have had 200,000 cavalry alone. The number of *mansabdar* officers is, however, known in minute detail, since it was recorded in army lists. In 1596 there were 1,803 *mansabdars* and by 1690 there were no less than 14,449. In 1648 Shah-jahan found that his army consisted – on paper – of 440,000 men, including 200,000 cavalry, 8,000 ordinary *mansabdars*, 7,000 élite *ahadis*, 40,000 infantry and artillerymen, plus 185,000 cavalry from the contingents of various princes and noblemen. Even this enormous figure excluded militias commanded by the local *Faujdars* and *Karoris*.

CAVALRY

Cavalry was always the most important element of the Mughul *lashkar* or army. It was divided into four basic parts. The best, or at least the highest paid and most elaborately equipped, were the élite *ahadi* 'gentlemen troopers'. Many of these had yet to receive a *mansab* rank. Akbar's *ahadis* were under the authority of a senior nobleman, and had their own *bakhshi* paymaster. Their main duty was to serve as aides to the Emperor, carrying important messages and guarding the palace. The pay (and status) of *ahadis* was lower than that of the lowest *mansabdar* officer but higher than that of the ordinary *tabinan* trooper.

Second came the *dakhilis* or 'supplementary troops', who were raised and paid by the state. *Dakhilis* under the direct command of the ruler himself were known as the *Wala Shahi* and often consisted of men who had followed him while he was a prince. Of these, a cavalry élite were called the *Tabinan-i Khasa-i Padshahi*, which, during Aurangzib's reign, numbered some 4,000 men. Most *dakhilis* were put under the command of various *mansabdars*. Some *dakhilis* were sent by the Emperor to serve under officers who were not otherwise permitted to recruit their own followers.

'Conqueror at the gate of a city' on a page from the Hamza Nama, 1567–82. This magnificent Mughul miniature shows an élite cavalryman and a foot soldier armed with jamdhar, a short-shafted axe, and using a sling. Note that the horseman has two swords in addition to a dagger, spear and archery equipment. (Photo: Susan Dirk, Seattle Art Museum, inv. 68.160)

The walls and gate of the Purana Qila'a fortress in Delhi built in the early 16th century. This is one of the best and earliest examples of Mughul fortification. It also incorporates a typical chatri 'kiosk' on top of one of the gate towers.

The troops recruited personally by the *mansabdars* formed the third class of cavalry. These followers were mostly ordinary *tabinan* cavalrymen. Their drill and standards of training varied considerably, as did their equipment. Their first loyalty was to the *mansabdar* who recruited them, yet they proved to be the most reliable element of the cavalry during Akbar's reign.

The fourth and final class of cavalry were the irregulars led by various autonomous or tributary chiefs. Many were Hindu *zamindars* from the indigenous Indian military class whose local authority was recognised by the Mughul government. Akbar was normally attended by 20 *zamindars* each with his own entourage. In return the *zamindars* paid the Mughuls regular tribute and contributed irregular military forces when needed. In the early days regular *tabinan* cavalry troopers tended to gravitate towards leaders of their own ethnic or cultural background: Afghan recruits normally served under Afghan *mansabdars*, Turks under Turks, and so on. Even when this broke down in later years, many units continued to have a proportion of men from the 'correct' ethnic origin.

The quality of troops was checked by a horse-branding system known as *dagh*, an ancient idea reintroduced during Akbar's military reforms. It was designed to prevent men from selling their horse and serving as infantry, or buying the cheapest mounts available. The Imperial brand was put on the animal's right haunch, the *mansabdar's* own brand on the left. At intervals a *tashiha* or 'verification' of men and horses was carried out during which a detailed description, known as a *chehra*, was made of the man's appearance and family background.

Little is known about the training of Mughul cavalry, though recruits certainly had to pass stiff tests of fitness and horsemanship. Thereafter training seems to have been an individual matter. Soldiers exercised at home using dumb-bells or heavy pieces of wood; in the rainy season they engaged in wrestling matches. Mughul archery training clearly involved shooting on foot as well as horseback; and Indian cavalry, particularly the Hindu Rajputs, were proud of their ability to fight as infantry when necessary. The typical Indian martial exercise was *kasarat*, which involved physical exercises as well as fencing with sword and buckler.

Horses

The importance of horses to an army made up primarily of cavalry is obvious. Throughout the Middle Ages large numbers of horses had been imported into India, mainly from Somalia, Arabia, Transoxania and Iran. As early as the time of Babur injured mounts were sent back from the sweltering plains of India to the cool mountain pastures of Afghanistan to recuperate. The Mughuls set up their own highly organised Imperial stables under a senior official called the *Atbegi*, each stable being run by a *daroga* assisted by *mushrif* accountants. Akbar raised the standard of horse breeding within

India so much that the horses of Cutch in Gujarat were eventually considered better even than the famous Arabian breeds.

The Mughuls seem to have valued strength and endurance above speed, perhaps because their cavalry made so much use of horse-armour. Some horses were trained to walk or jump forwards on their hind legs to give a rider the height he needed to attack a war elephant. Above all, a Mughul war-horse had to be able to stop dead and wheel around on its hind legs. The Persians, however, considered that the Indians crushed the spirit of their horses by making them too obedient.

INFANTRY

Mughul infantry never had the prestige of the cavalry but they still played a vital role. Most were ill-armed peasants or townsfolk levied by local Muslim *mansabdars* or Hindu *zamindars*. The only professional infantry were the matchlockmen, the best of whom seem to have come from the lower Ganges Plain and Bengal. In the early days, however, only a quarter of the *dakhili* or ordinary infantry were armed with matchlocks; the remainder were infantry archers, or served as carpenters, blacksmiths, water-carriers and pioneers. Other infantry were recruited from the Rohillas of the foothills around Rawalpindi. They were also sent to settle newly conquered territories in central and southern India. By the 16th century other warriors were coming from the mountainous deserts of Baluchistan; they fought as infantry archers and on camel-back. Ethiopians are also sometimes mentioned, though mostly as palace eunuchs or members of the Delhi police force.

During Akbar's reign many groups in and around the palace were categorised as infantry. These included: *darban* porters; *Khidmatiyyahs*, who were special units of guards apparently recruited from 'thieves and highwaymen'; *mewrahs* or running messengers recruited in what is now Rajasthan; *shamsherbaz* or 'court gladiators'; *pahluwans*, 'court wrestlers'; *chelahs*, royal slaves; and finally *kuhar*, 'bearers' in charge of man-carrying litters. Almost certainly the most exotic 'infantry' were the *Urdu-*

begis, a unit of armed women who guarded the Imperial harem.

Mughul infantry forces were under the overall command of an officer known as the *Darogha*. Akbar's *banduqchis* or matchlockmen, numbered 12,000 in five grades, the most senior being the *mirdadah* 'leader of ten'. This was the only NCO rank in the Mughul army, and was distinct from the *dahbashi* 'commander of ten' which was a *mansabdar* officer rank. The rest of the *banduqchi* matchlockmen were divided into four 'pay grades'. The only other infantry rank was an officer known as the *Khidmat Ray* in command of Akbar's *Khidmatiyyah* palace guards.

At the bottom end of the military scale was the largely Hindu *bumi* local militia. Somewhat better equipped were police forces organised at village, district and urban level. Those in the cities were under a *Kotwal*, who had considerable authority; he was assisted by men in charge of each section of town, as well as spies and detectives. Though the *Kotwal's* main duty was to preserve law and order, he was also expected to expel religious fanatics, arrange special illuminations for religious festivals, help defend the town in case of enemy attack, and even to stop widows from being forced to commit *sati* or Hindu ritual suicide if they didn't really want to. Each *sarkar* rural district was responsible for its own militia contingent, and here most of the forces responsible for maintaining order were under the authority of a local *Faujdar*. Though he had great power, the *Faujdar* also had onerous responsibilities. These included compensating any traveller who was robbed in daylight. (If the theft took place at night it was regarded as the victim's fault for being out after dark!)

The equipment of Mughul infantry was very varied. Matchlocks were preferred, even by the military élite, as they proved to be more reliable

▶ '*Victory of Kutb al Din Khan at Gujarat*', in the Akbar Nama, *c.1590. Kutb al Din's cavalry and elephant troops are shown with the full variety of Mughul arms and armour, wearing mail or lamellar. Their horse-armour appears even more decorative. The elephants in the* foreground are fully armoured, but those carrying drummers on the upper part of the picture are unarmoured. Also note the two Mughul standard-bearers at the top of the picture. (Victoria & Albert Museum, Ms. 2-1896, 108/ 117, London)

This well-known miniature from the Akbar Nama shows Mughul artillery bombarding the fort of Ranthambhor. In the foreground another heavy gun is dragged forward by a team of bullocks. (Victoria & Albert Museum, Ms. 2–1896, 721 117)

than flintlocks in India's dust and damp. Otherwise most foot soldiers carried swords, shields, assorted spears, daggers, bows and sometimes crossbows. The powerful composite bow of Central Asian origin had been known in India for a thousand years but suffered from the local climate; as a result the *kamtha* or simple bow – similar in design to the medieval English longbow – remained in use despite its much inferior performance. Muslim India also developed a 'water-proof' type of composite bow suitable for the Indian climate. The main role of Mughul infantry was in the siege warfare which played such an important part in Mughul military campaigns. European travellers, however, considered that even the Emperor's own matchlockmen were not well trained.

ELEPHANTS

War elephants were the most characteristic, though certainly not the most important, element of the Mughul army. The majority were females, used to carry baggage and to pull guns; a smaller number of male elephants were trained to fight. Western observers have consistently denigrated the value of elephants in warfare. However, Babur himself

stated that three or four elephants could haul a large *qazan* mortar which otherwise needed four or five hundred men. (On the other hand he noted that one elephant ate as much as fifteen camels.)

The *Ain-i Akbari*, written in Akbar's reign, also eulogised the Mughul war elephant: '*This wonderful animal is in bulk and strength like a mountain, and in courage and ferocity like a lion. It adds materially to the pomp of a king and to the success of a conqueror. Experienced men of India put the value of a good elephant equal to 500 horses, and they believe that when it is guided by a few bold men armed with matchlocks one such elephant is worth double that number.*'

The main functions of war elephants seem to have been their use either as rallying points, or as platforms to display the army's banners and to give commanders enough height to see what was going on. (This could, however, make Mughul commanders vulnerable: one invading Persian ruler said of them early in the 18th century that, '*In the day of the battle they ride on an elephant and make themselves a target for everybody.*')

In 1526 Babur described how Indian war elephants attacked enemy cavalry, crushing many horses so that their riders had to escape on foot. The great beasts were very difficult to kill, though they could more easily be driven off. Akbar

Painting by Sur Das, one of the most famous Mughul Court artists, showing a Mughul and his attendant fighting a lion on elephant-back, c.1605. A typically unarmoured Hindu foot-soldier also wields a broad straight sword and carries a small round shield. (Location unknown)

abandoned the old belief that it was unlucky to breed elephants in stables. He set up several studs, where local *Faujdars* were responsible for training the animals, starting when they were ten years old and accustoming them to the sound of gunfire. Soon Akbar had matchlockmen and archers riding into battle on their backs. Some years later armoured elephants even carried small cannon.

ARTILLERY

During the early 16th century the Portuguese noted that the Mughuls possessed very large guns. They also noted that Indian bronze cannon were superior to those of iron. Many types of artillery were already in use, including *firingi* 'European' light field guns, *zarbzan*, which were operated by two men, and *tufang* matchlocks. Babur's heaviest weapon seems to have been a mortar with a range of 1,600 paces. Some years later Humayun's army was said to include 700 light cannon pulled by bullocks as well as 21 heavy guns.

Under Akbar there were great advances in artillery and the Mughul Empire was, alongside the Ottoman Empire, the leading Muslim state in terms of gunnery. The Emperor set up new factories and was said to test all new guns. Akbar was particularly keen on matchlocks and was reputedly a fine shot. He was credited with inventing guns that could be dismantled on the march, weapons with 17 barrels that could be fired with a single match, a *gajnal* heavy musket for use on elephant-back, and even an oxen-powered 'wheel' which could clean 17 matchlock barrels at once.

Mughul guns now included at least two types of matchlock, the standard barrel being about four feet long, the larger six feet. The *dhamakah* and the *ramjanaki* were forms of field-gun, the *arghun* a multi-barrelled weapon. During the later Mughul period an improved ox-drawn gun-cart known as the *rahkala* also appeared. Early in the 18th century iron-bound wooden cannon were used by Sikh rebels against the Mughuls, being regarded as half as effective as metal guns. Other Mughul fire-weapons included the *ghabarah* mortar or its bomb, the *deg* mortar, the *huqqah-i atish*, which was prob-

ably a large earthenware grenade, the *handi* clay grenade thrown by a sling, *chadar*, bundles of inflammable material, and *ban* rockets.

Rockets, in fact, became increasingly popular from the mid-16th century. Mughul rockets had a range of up to 1,000 yards and up to ten could be mounted and fired from camel-back. Some had explosive heads, while others skimmed along the ground to frighten the enemy's horses. A British officer named Congreve saw such weapons used in India in 1806, and went on to develop his own (marginally) improved versions to be used against Napoleon's forces.

Babur was the first Indian ruler to organise the artillery into a separate unit within his army. Thereafter cannon and their gunners remained strictly under state control as a department of the Imperial Household commanded by a senior officer known as the *Mir-i Atish* or *Darugha-i Tup-khana*. By the 18th century this man had become very important. Beneath him the artillery officers were divided into the same *mansab* ranks as the cavalry, each unit being led by a *hazari*. Most master-gunners were Ottoman Turks, though there were also Arabs, Indians, Portuguese and Dutchmen. From

◄ *A Mughul Prince painted by Muhammad Ali, c.1610–15. In addition to its magnificent harness, this nobleman's horse carries a small drum on the front of its saddle and gilded leather cones around its red henna-stained ankles. (Location unknown)*

► *'The battle of Sarnath', from the* Akbar Nama, *c.1590. Once again Akbar's heavily armoured cavalry élite and their horses wear elaborately decorated armour. Most of the Mughuls have cloth-covered, probably scale-lined tunics. The man at the centre also has laminated arm and leg defences in addition to the plated vambraces which protect the lower arms of every warrior in this picture. (Victoria & Albert Museum, Ms. 2-1896, 106/117)*

the mid-17th century European mercenary artillerymen reached very high rank within the Mughul army; one Dutch gunner is known to have served in India for 16 years before returning home a rich man.

Mughul artillery probably reached its peak under Aurangzib in the second half of the 17th century, but by then European arms merchants were already selling inferior guns to various Indian rulers. Later Mughul rulers also loved very big bronze cannon. These were heavily decorated and had heroic-sounding names, but they were designed primarily to impress an enemy with their size and noise rather than their actual destructiveness. The artillery's rate of fire remained very slow, ordinary cannon shooting once every 15 minutes while the giant guns fired maybe once every 45 minutes.

LOGISTICS

In addition to gun-foundries, the first Mughul rulers also set up arsenals to manufacture arms and armour. By the 17th century these had evolved into a sophisticated system of *karkhanas* to produce military material, and *thanah* bases serving as regional supply depots. Other more specialised arsenals in the Imperial Palace included one for the *qur* flags, banners and musical instruments under the authority of a *qurbegi*.

The Mughul transport system was well organised. Baggage animals included Bactrian camels, dromedaries and oxen as well as elephants. Yet there was no real commissariat, most men buying food for themselves and their horses in the 'military bazaar' which followed every army. Only the Emperor's own household troops were served by special military kitchens. Mughul medical services may have been inferior to those seen in earlier Muslim armies, most of the wounded having to rely on their own relatives for treatment after a battle.

The River Ganges had always been a major communications artery and Akbar used it to transport huge quantities of war material during campaigns in Bengal. Akbar also appointed a *Mir Bahr* 'river commander' in charge of all river transport, boatmen, sailors, wharves, ferries, and tolls. The Indian Ocean, meanwhile, was a

Akbar's troops on a miniature showing 'Akbar visiting the Shrine of Muin al Din', in the Akbar Nama, c.1590. In the lower left corner a soldier carries a massive, highly decorated matchlock musket, while in the centre two bare-chested Hindu warriors have decorated shields and typical straight swords with blades broadening towards the points. (Victoria & Albert Museum, Ms. 2-1896, 23/ 117)

remarkably peaceful place until the Europeans arrived. It was full of large ships, some of which were made to serve as military transports during coastal campaigns. The only real Mughul navy was a fleet of 750 ships which attempted to protect the Bengali coast from Burmese and European pirates. During the 17th century a more successful navy, operated by the semi-independent *Sidis* or governors of Janjira Island south of Bombay, helped the Mughuls against the Marathas.

THE LATER MUGHULS

As the Mughul Empire declined so did the army. The fighting skills of troops based at the centre of the Empire declined in comparison with those of troops stationed in rebellious provinces, which, by the 17th century, were already starting to break away from government control. Europeans who visited mid-17th century India described Mughul soldiers as brave but undisciplined and liable to panic. Jealousy between senior commanders was an even more serious problem, as was decreasing loyalty to the Emperor. The real problem probably lay in the complexity of Akbar's military structure.

Jahangir tried to simplify it, but only succeeded in making the situation worse.

When Shah-jahan came to the throne he found his army was far larger on paper than in reality. Senior officers lent each other troops to make up numbers before reviews, while others rounded up untrained men from the bazaars and mounted them on any available pony. Shah-jahan recognised the situation and, in 1630, reduced the army's official size in line with what actually existed. At the same time he also reduced officer salaries by paying them for only part of the year. Competent and incompetent *mansabdars* were being paid equal amounts, so Shah-jahan introduced yet another variation to the ranking structure. This was the *do-aspa-sih-aspa* 'two or three horses' number added to the existing *zat* and *sawar* ranks as reward for good conduct: in effect it meant that some officers were given the money to maintain additional horses. Shah-jahan also instructed that if a *mansabdar* was serving in his home province he must maintain a military contingent one-third the size of the *sawar* number, but if he was posted elsewhere he need only maintain a quarter of this figure. If such an officer was sent the other side of the Afghan mountains he need only maintain one-fifth the troops of his *sawar*.

The Mughul army still took part in huge campaigns with some success, but by the late 17th century Aurangzib faced an increasingly effective enemy from within India: the Hindu Marathas. By the end of his reign the cost of these great southern campaigns broke the Mughul Empire's financial back, and the centralised and highly structúred army fell apart. Under Aurangzib's successors the Mughul army was made up mostly of units maintained by great noblemen who used them to pursue their own political rivalries.

Recruitment for the late Mughul army was even more varied than it had been in earlier days. By the 18th century people of humble social rank were rising to real military power. These included both Hindu and Muslim 'tax farmers', who combined local military authority with considerable money-making skills. Many had their own small military forces, and their relationship with provincial governors and the Emperor tended to be based on mercenary contracts rather than traditional loyalties. The troops themselves included cavalry from Afghanistan and what is now northern and central Pakistan, though the most reliable seem to have been the Hindu Rajputs. By the 18th century the most effective Mughul infantry were provided by the Arabs, recruited probably in Oman and the Yemen. These were famed for fencing skills which are still reflected in the traditional tribal dances of south-eastern Arabia; and they are said to have charged to the roar of small drums, making acrobatic leaps and even somersaults to frighten their foes.

THE SUCCESSOR STATES

Various new states emerged from the fragmenting Mughul Empire in the 18th century. These included resurgent Hindu kingdoms in southern India; 'rebel' states set up by Jats and Sikhs close to Delhi; new Muslim Conquest states in the north-west; and virtually independent Mughul provinces such as Oudh in the north, Bengal in the east and Hyderabad in the south. Some provinces had been ruled by *Nazim* or *Nizam* governors for decades. While the *Nazims* were responsible for defence and local order, another official called the *Diwan* was responsible for financial affairs. Early in the 18th century a single man became both *Nazim* and *Diwan* of Bengal; he founded a semi-independent dynasty of *Nawabs* – a term which has entered English as 'Nabob'.

The *Nawab's* army included both Muslims and Hindus but it tended to be a fragmented force whose loyalties were to local commanders. Such local leaders included Muslim *Faujdars*, most of whom lived in frontier areas and were, by the early 18th century, largely appointed by the *Nawab*

'Jahangir suppresses a rebellion', from the Kevorkian Album, c.1623. The extravagantly dressed Mughul emperor has a small dagger in his belt, a curved sabre and a massive round shield on his left hip. Most interesting, however, is his matchlock musket with its curved supporting fork folded forwards. (Location unknown)

Complete mail-and-plate elephant armour from late Mughul India, probably 18th century. (Royal Armouries, Tower of London)

rather than the Emperor. Hindu *zamindars* also had local authority in many parts of Bengal and the bulk of their troops were Hindu *paik* infantry. Their territories, called *zamindari*, could be as big as 13,000 square miles, and the *Zamindar* of Burdwan, for example, had his own 30,000-strong militia plus full-time household troops. Other elements in the fragmented forces of Bengal were *ghatwal* frontier guards or military settlers given land in return for protecting the borders; and the *chaukidars*, who were given small pieces of land in return for acting as village watchmen.

Developments in the south ran a similar course. Here the *Nizam* of Hyderabad also won a great deal of autonomy and was more successful in carving out a strong quasi-independent Muslim state with its own powerful army. By the early 18th century the military forces of the *Nizam* relied on heavily armoured cavalry and heavy (if cumbersome) field artillery. Despite many successes the *Nizam* of Hyderabad's army was, however, generally unable to deal with the famous light cavalry raiders of the Hindu Marathas.

Complete mail-and-plate horse armour from Mughul northern India, 17th century. (Royal Armouries, Tower of London)

MUGHUL WARFARE

In the early days Mughul strategy relied on a combination of élite cavalry and a series of well-garrisoned defensive strongholds. Traditional Mughul tactics based on heavy cavalry and war elephants were always more effective on the plains of northern India than in the hills of the Deccan or the marshes of Bengal. The Mughuls normally took few chances and their campaigns relied on elaborate preparations and overwhelming force. In the 17th century the Mughul general Jai Singh adopted a traditionally careful Mughul strategy against the Marathas, only trying to capture those enemy fortresses which he could then hold and use to strangle the Marathas' movements.

Wars were normally conducted during the dry season, though Akbar did carry out at least one campaign during the monsoon despite flooded rivers and torrential rain. Aurangzib certainly used the great rivers when campaigning in Assam and Cooch Bihar. Combined land, sea and river operations became of vital importance during the middle and later Mughul periods.

The army on the march

Among the many things which astonished 16th-century European visitors to India was the appearance of the Mughul army on campaign. Father Antonio Monserrate, a Jesuit missionary, noted that the Mughul host looked small while in camp but enormous on the march. On the other hand Monserrate criticised what he saw as the elaborate and unwieldy impedimenta that the Mughul army carried. He also described how heralds went ahead of the main force, warning minor rulers not to attempt resistance. Even so the army paid for all provisions it consumed while marching through friendly or neutral territory.

Generally speaking, in the 16th century the army tried to avoid marching across the great plains, where water was scarce, and kept instead to the foothills with their streams. It also avoided the mountains, where it was vulnerable to ambush, and where there were always difficulties getting an army through high passes without confusion. Mughul armies were preceded by a large force of pioneers to clear the way, to repair bridges and, where necessary, to make rafts. Such support troops were commanded by a senior military engineer, who also stationed officers to serve as marshals at river crossings. Local governors and subordinate rulers were expected to provide boats at crossings when needed.

The Mughul army marched behind a screen of scouts. Information from Aurangzib's time states that the heavy artillery was sent first along with the advance guard (a time-saving measure used also in most European armies of this period, since the guns were the slowest part of the army). On the way home the heavy guns brought up the rear. The advance guard was followed by the baggage-train: camels and elephants carrying the Imperial Treasury, the Emperor's hunting establishment with its dogs, the official records carried by camels, elephants and carts; more camels bearing water supplies for the Court, the imperial kitchen on camel-back, a herd of cattle for milk, cooks, and the imperial wardrobe with its armoury carried by mules . . . The amount of imperial baggage taken on campaign reached an extreme under Aurangzib,

though there was good cause for such extravagance: displays of imperial splendour were intended to awe an enemy into submission without a fight.

The baggage was followed by the main bulk of the army. First came the cavalry, then the Emperor in person and his harem with infantry guarding each flank, then the light artillery as a rearguard. Finally, hordes of camp followers trailed behind. In Akbar's day the army marched to the rhythm of a single slow drum and discipline on the march was very strict. Babur recalled how he made an accurate count of the army's numbers as they crossed a river, finding the result a lot smaller than he had expected.

Mughul imperial tents in a 19th-century engraving from an early 17th-century copy of the Ain-i Akbari *manuscript: (1) bargah pavilion, (2) duashyanah manzil two-storied tent, (3) chubin rawati raised tent, (4) yak-surughah single-pole tent, (5) dusurughah two-pole tent, (6) mandal awning, (7) ajaibi special awning. (After Blochmann)*

The army in camp

The best site for an army camp had its own source of drinking water, access to a good supply of firewood, and was also defensible. At night it was protected by *tilayah* pickets from the advance-guard, and by *shab* patrols led by *kotwal* officers, who communicated with trumpets.

Akbar's imperial camp or *gulalbar* was a gated enclosure one hundred yards square at the centre of the army camp. Next door was a circular enclosure containing 12 divisions and a state tent as audience halls. On top of his other reforms, Akbar was credited with inventing a new layout for the main camp which was said to make it easier for soldiers to find their way around. The noblemen's tents surrounded the imperial enclosure, with the soldier's tents clustered, in turn, around them. A burning beacon on a tall pole guided stragglers home at night and served as a rallying point in case of attack. The artillery was assembled on the side of the camp that faced any anticipated enemy attack. To avoid overcrowding the troops were separated into *ordu* divisions, with separate bazaars for the followers of each senior officer.

Cautious commanders like Babur camped in battle array if an enemy was near, with infantry stationed all around at a bow-shot's distance. Trusted members of his household inspected the defences once every night, and if a man was not found at his allotted post his nose was slit open. Field fortifications and camps were defended by ditches and artificial hedges made of the thorniest branches available, as well as incorporating gun emplacements protected by sandbags. From the early 18th century camps were also defended by two-metre-high parapets inside the ditch, with guns and mortars mounted on top.

Mughul battle tactics

According to Mughul military theorists the best position for a battle was with hills to the rear, on smooth ground that had no stones to hurt the horses' feet, neither too dusty, nor too sandy, nor too marshy; neither too close nor too far from habitation; and with its own water supply. Babur's autobiography also states that it was impossible to arrange the battle array in mountains or jungle, the men having to reach open ground first. A senior *bakhshi* officer was responsible for drawing up a battle plan and for assigning the leadership of divisions. He would then present this plan to the Emperor for approval, normally the day before the battle.

Mughul commanding officers communicated with those in charge of various divisions through adjutants known as *tawaci, yasawal* or *sazawal*, or by using drums, flags or couriers. Mughul insignia evolved out of those previously used by Timurid rulers. The *tuq* with its pendant yak-tails was, for example, of pagan Central Asian origin. The lion and sun motif had been used by the Chagatay Mongol rulers of Samarkand before Babur adopted

'*Attendant of a Prince out hunting*', made at Golconda in south-central India, c.1615. Note the typically southern India straight khanda *sword, the hilt of which incorporates a knuckle-guard. (British Library, Ms. Johnson 67.3)*

it. Akbar had an array of particularly elaborate insignia, including several types of *aurang* throne, the *chart* parasol adorned with jewels, the *saiban* or oval sunshade made of brocade, the *kaukabah* banner, five *alam* standards each in their own scarlet bag, the *chatrtoq* which was smaller than an *alam* with yak-tails, the *tumantoq*, which was longer than the *chatrtoq*, and the *jhanda*, which was an Indian flag.

Military music was even more highly developed. Battles would start at a signal given by large *naubat* drums, horns and battle-cries. Other military instruments included *naqqarah* kettle-drums, *dankah* small drums, cymbals and various trumpets. The battle-cry of Muslim troops was typically *Allahu Akbar* ('God is Most Powerful'), *Din Din Muhammad* ('The Faith, the Faith of Muhammad'); or *Ya Mu'in* ('Oh Divine Helper'). The Hindus for their part often shouted *Gopal Gopal*, which was one of the names of the god Krishna. To avoid confusion during battle, units would further identify themselves with pre-arranged passwords.

Babur's tactical ideas were largely based on Tamerlane's of a century earlier. The army had a *baranghar* right wing, *jawanghar* left wing, *harawal* advance guard, and *gul* centre. Under the later Mughuls this basic structure was elaborated to include: *qalawuri* scouts, an *iftali* vanguard, *qarawal* skirmishers, *juzah-i harawal* advance post of the advance guard, *iltmish* advance guard of the centre, *tarah* wings of the centre, *chandawul* rearguard, *saqah* protective rear ranks of any division, *taulqamah* ambush troops, and *nasaqchi* military police to stop men from retreating without orders.

But it was the adoption of field artillery that brought the greatest tactical innovations. For his great victory at Panipat, Babur linked the gun carts with rawhide ropes. Between each cart were five or six large mantlets behind which the matchlock infantry stood ready to fire; other infantry were also drawn up behind the carts and mantlets. Babur's right flank rested on the suburbs of Panipat, his left flank being guarded by a ditch and artificial hedge. Separated at a distance of an arrow-shot along the front were sally points, each with one to two hundred cavalry posted ready to charge. In a later battle there were too few gun carts to cover the entire front, so Babur had rawhide ropes stretched between wooden tripods (which could also be mounted on wheels). When Babur's army advanced

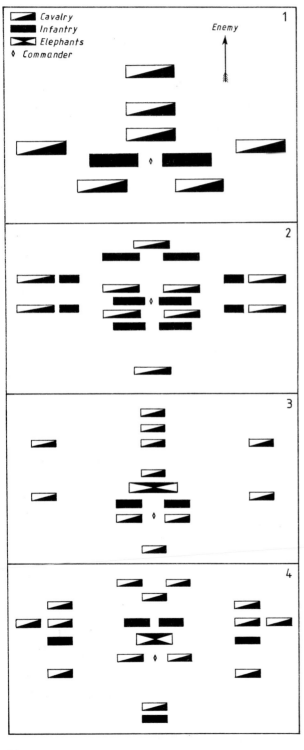

Mughul battle formations according to the Shah-jahan Nama: (1) five division system, (2) seven division system, (3) nine division system, (4) 12 division system.

The campaigns of Babur,
early 16th C
1: Babur
2: Turco-Mongol yigit ('brave')
3: Afghan infantryman with baggage camel

1

2

3

A

The conquest, loss & reconquest
of India, mid-16th C
1: Mirza officer,
  Mughul cavalry
2: Northern Indian
  Muslim cavalryman
3: Muslim bunduqchi
  (matchlockman)

B

Akbar's cavalry, late 16th C to early 17th C 1: Mansabdar (officer) 2: Tabinan (trooper) 3: Afghan light cavalry leader

C

Akbar's infantry and artillery
1: Infantry officer
2: Artilleryman
3: Indian bumi (militiaman)

D

Akbar's elephants
1: Senior commander with elephant
2: Fighting elephant with crew
3: Jesuit missionary

E

The Age of Empire: mid- to late 17th C
1: Emperor Shah-jahan
2: Imperial guardsman   3: Court trumpeter

F

Court life, late 17th C to early 18th C
1: Mughul prince
2: Heavy cavalryman from Hyderabad
3: Mughul court lady

G

Fall of the Mughuls, early to mid-18th C
1: Rajput Zamindar 3: Maratha infantryman
2: Maratha light cavalryman

H

to attack, the infantry sometimes went first still carrying their mantlets, until the Mughul cavalry suddenly charged ahead. It was also possible for the entire defensive front of carts and rawhide ropes to move forward, as it did for two miles at the victorious battle of Kanwa in 1527.

Most full-scale battles started with an artillery duel followed by successive cavalry charges carried out first by one wing of the army, then by the other. Fighting normally started in the morning and stopped in the evening, though it might continue until nightfall if an army hoped to retreat under the cover of darkness. The main aim of any Indian army was to reach and overthrow the enemy commander on his elephant; if this could be done the opposition invariably collapsed.

Other modes of warfare included feigned flight to draw the enemy into an ambush; placing matchlock infantry in defiles to kill an enemy leader; the multiple impersonation of a commander to minimise the danger of him being targeted in battle; and *qazaqi* raiding by light cavalry (the originally turkish word *qazaqi* was westernised to become 'Cossack'). On occasion horsemen dismounted to attack the unprotected bellies of armoured elephants with large daggers. By the late 17th century some Mughul cavalrymen had matchlocks as well as bows; various commanders wrote despatches asking for mounted musketeers to face Maratha infantry, but the Mughul army was never to have enough.

In the early days almost all tactical movement was left to the cavalry, but Akbar did attempt to develop mobile field artillery and this became quite important under Aurangzib. The heavier artillery could not, of course, be moved during a battle and in case of defeat would simply be spiked. Elsewhere the silence of the guns could fool an enemy into premature attack.

SIEGE WARFARE

Siege engineering and fortification had been highly developed in pre-Islamic India. On the northern plains defences tended to be raised on artificial mounds often surrounded by water-filled ditches or even marshes. In the rockier terrain of central India

Mughul guards and standard-bearers in a miniature showing 'Shah-jahan receiving three officers', Shah-jahan Nama, 1656-7. The standards carried by these men include the Panja or 'Hand of Fatima', and others portraying figures. (Ms. P. 188, f.72v, The Royal Collection © 1993 Her Majesty the Queen)

fortresses were built on naturally inaccessible sites. In Sind, Punjab and Bengal, where good stone was scarce, brick was used, while in Kashmir some defences were of wood. Many of these existing fortifications were greatly strengthened by the invading Mughuls. Babur also brought with him new ideas from Central Asian and Persian military architecture. Even after the arrival of the Mughuls the main concern in the design of Indian fortresses was, in all cases, the provision of an adequate water supply.

Traditional Indian mud wall forts, though primitive, proved their worth against the Mughuls' new gunpowder artillery, their walls absorbing shot rather than shattering. They were also easy to raze if an area was about to be lost to an enemy, and as quickly and cheaply replaced. Forts on the northern

Agra Fort, late 16th century. This huge fortress has a typical series of walls, one behind the other and each of increasing height, with which Mughul military architects attempted to confront the threat of gunpowder artillery.

plains were often surrounded by thick brakes of bamboo capable of stopping or at least of slowing cannon balls; some had cultivated 'walls' of cactus-like prickly pears up to 20 feet high which resisted fire.

Mughul castle designers rarely used outworks: to make a citadel stronger they simply added more and higher walls, giving the stepped effect most clearly seen in the famous triple-walled fortress at Agra (see above). Until the end of the 16th century the other main features were towers which projected only a short distance from the main wall, the strong slope or batter of this wall, covered galleries within the walls, external galleries on the wall's outer face, and *chatris* kiosks over the gates. During the 17th century Mughul fortification tended to have partly solid semicircular towers, many small box-like machicolations on these towers, and even more numerous loopholes in the wall often protected by stone hoods for downwards firing. Fortified barbettes were then added for additional guns. In

some places high internal bastions were erected for defensive artillery. Old walls were straightened and strengthened while many more embrasures for light cannon were made high in such walls. The Deccan was already more dotted with castles than the rest of India and here Mughul fortifications were reproduced on a smaller scale by many mountain-top rulers.

During the late 17th and early 18th centuries various aspects of military architecture continued to be used purely decoratively, long after they had any real defensive purpose; later Mughul towers were more for display than strength, and served as platforms from which a ruler could address his people.

The Mughul sciences of siege and counter-siege were similarly highly developed. As early as 1495, in Farghana in Central Asia, Babur's autobiography recalled extensive counter-mining and the use of smoke to drive enemy miners from their tunnels. On one occasion the defenders forced an enemy back by filling their mines with water. In India itself the Rajputs defended their castles against Babur's men by hurling rocks and fire on their heads. During one siege, a brazier was used to heat an iron

The massive frontier fortress at Daulatabad in the Deccan was originally a Hindu castle. It was rebuilt by the Muslim Sultans of Delhi in the 14th century. The Mughul Emperor Shah-jahan captured it in 1633 and added a palace to the summit of the citadel. (A) Bastion on the inner wall of the moat; (B) Main fortified gateway; (C) Steps to the Citadel and Shah-jahan's Pavilion.

(A)

(B)

(C)

door so the enemy could not push it open. External gates would also be studded with large iron spikes against the elephants which besiegers used as living battering-rams.

Stone-throwing mangonels were still in use as late as the 16th century; by then, however, cannon were becoming more important. During Akbar's siege of the huge Rajput fortress of Chitor in 1567 the Mughuls had three gun batteries, plus a large mortar which shot 40-pound balls; this massive weapon was manufactured on site, on the top of a neighbouring hill to avoid having to drag its barrel up the steep slopes. Other siege devices included the *pasheb* or raised platform of sandbags; the *sarkob* or *damdama* which was a fixed tower of wood, stone or mud to overlook an enemy's defences; the *sabat* or covered trench; the *seeba* or mobile tower; the *zem pey* suspension bridge of rope and wood; the *jhala* raft on inflated skins which could carry up to 80 men, the *zeenah pae* or broad scaling ladder, the *narduban* ordinary scaling ladder, and the *kamand* rope ladder; and the *turah* heavy mantlet.

Some Mughul siege work appears to have been colossal in scale. A *sabat* attack-trench could, it was said, be wide enough for ten horsemen riding side-by-side, and deep enough to hide completely a man riding on an elephant. Nonetheless, the Mughuls seem to have been much less effective in making breaches than were their European contemporaries. Even Akbar's mighty army often had to resort to bribery to bring a siege to an end; in a number of cases sieges lasted several years.

THE PLATES

A: The campaigns of Babur, early 16th century

The army of the early Mughuls was mostly Turco-Mongol in appearance and structure. Here the first Mughul conqueror, Barbur, is depicted crossing an Afghan pass in winter, looking for new lands to conquer.

A1: Babur

Babur wears Turkish costume including a *burk* felt cap, a fur-lined silk coat, loose silk trousers and decorated riding boots. The steel *dastana* vambraces protecting his arms have extensions to cover the back of the hands. In addition to his archery equipment he is armed with a dagger with a jade grip, and a slightly curved sabre of late Timurid type; a large flanged mace is thrust beneath the saddle. (Main sources: manuscript from Bukhara, 16th century, British Library, London, Ms. John. 56.12; 'Battle scene', Persian c.1520, Royal Scottish Museum, Edinburgh; Persian sabre, 15th century, Topkapi Museum, Istanbul; 'Sultan Mirza visiting

a hermit', Herat 1484, British Library, Ms. Or. 6810.)

A2: Turco-Mongol yigit ('brave')

Beneath his iron helmet this warrior has a quilted *duwalgha burki* arming cap. His *qalmaq jiba* heavy lamellar cuirass was sometimes described as a 'Chinese' form of armour; its iron lamellae were of different sizes for various parts of the body. His forearms are protected by normal *dastana* vambraces while his legs are partially covered with lamellae and mail and a small bronze dome to cover the knee. A cotton-bound spiral-cane shield hangs from his saddle. His horse's *kichin* horse-armour consists of six sheets of fabric covered hardened leather lamellae and a head piece made of a bronze frame covered with hardened leather. (Main sources: Persian helmet, late 15th cent., Nat. Mus., Copenhagen; 'Sultan Mirza visiting a hermit', Herat 1484, Brit. Lib., Ms. Or. 6810; *Tarikh-i khandan-i Timuria*, India, early 16th cent., Khuda Bux Lib.; dagger, Persia early 16th cent, Royal Armoury, Stockholm.)

A3: Afghan infantryman with baggage camel

Here the turban has been folded in a loose manner fashionable in late 15th-century eastern Islam. The man also wears a sheepskin *postin* coat, and his boots are of fur-lined *charuq* moccasin type. His weaponry consists of a large spiral cane shield and an eastern

Mughul miniature showing 'Shah-jahan receiving three officers', Shah-jahan Nama, 1656–7. On the left, one man has a small musket over his shoulder, its mechanism protected by a cloth bag. In the centre two officers carry maces. (Ms. P. 188, f.72v, The Royal Collection © 1993 Her Majesty the Queen)

Islamic sabre, plus a bow without a bowcase (as was normal for foot-soldiers) and an infantry-style quiver. The Bactrian two-humped camel was one of the most important baggage animals in the early Mughul army. (Main sources: manuscript, Persia 1499–1500, Topkapi Library, Ms. Haz. 831, Istanbul; *Muhr-i Mushari* manuscript, Bukhara 1523, Freer Gall., inv. 32.6, Washington; *Khamseh of Nizami*, Herat c.1493, British Library, Ms. 25900; *Khamseh of Nizami*, Tabriz c.1540, Fogg Art Museum, Boston.)

B: The conquest, loss and reconquest of India, mid-16th century

Most battles of the early conquest period were between Muslim and Muslim rather than Muslim and Hindu. We show here a combat between two Mughuls and a cavalryman from the Muslim sultanate which ruled northern India before Babur's invasion.

B1: Mirza officer, Mughul cavalry

Red became the 'uniform' colour for men serving under the Mughul Emperor's immediate command. This man carries a gilded bronze standard with three yak-tails. His armour consists of decorated iron *dastana* vambraces and a mail shirt beneath a fabric-covered scale-lined cuirass. A bronze disc on his chest would have covered a strap securing this cuirass. Elaborately decorated saddles and harness became a feature of Mughul élite cavalry. (Main sources: *Fitzwilliam Album*, Mughul manuscript c.1555–60, Fitzwilliam Mus., inv. PD 72-1948, Cambridge; *Hamza Nama*, Mughul manuscript c.1562–77, Seattle Art Mus, inv. 68.160, Seattle; *Hamza Romance*, Mughul manuscript c.1555–80, Museum für Kunst und Industrie, Vienna.)

B2: Muslim cavalryman from northern India

The cavalry élite of northern India wore highly decorated armour before the coming of the

'The surrender of Kandahar' in the Padshah Nama, *1640–45. From the mid-16th century onwards Mughul miniatures start to portray Mughul troops in very different costume, arms and armour. Heavy, elaborate armours have been replaced by lighter mail-and-plate cuirasses supplemented by quilted collars and plate vambraces. Horse-armour is also much rarer, though one does appear in the lower left corner of this illustration. (Ms. 3318, Musée Guimet, Paris)*

Mughuls. This man's iron helmet is gilded while his cuirass consists of alternating rows of polished bronze lames and iron mail. His leg defences and horse-armour are made in the same way. Thrust into his belt is a large and characteristically Indian *jamdhar* dagger and he also carries a straight Indian *khanda* sword. (Main sources: *Babur Nama*, Mughul manuscript c.1598, Nat. Mus., Ms. 50.326, New Delhi; *Razm Nama*, Mughul manuscript c.1582–6, City Palace Mus., Jaipur.)

B3: Muslim bunduqchi (matchlockman)

The costume of Mughul infantry was basically that of ordinary peasants or artisans. This man has an Indian *jamdhar* dagger in addition to his matchlock musket. He wears a bullet- and cartridge-pouch belt, and is protected by a large wooden mantlet. (Main sources: *Ghengiz Khan Nama*, Mughul manuscript c.1596, Nat. Lib., Tehran; *Babur Nama*, Mughul manuscript, c.1598, Musée Guimet, Paris; *Babur Nama*, Mughul manuscript c.1598, Nat. Mus., Ms. 50.326, New Delhi.)

C: Akbar's cavalry, late 16th–early 17th centuries

Cavalry always formed the élite of the Mughul army and was at its most splendid and effective under Akbar, the grandson of Babur.

C1: Mansabdar (cavalry officer)

As a member of the Emperor Akbar's military élite this man is kitted in a magnificent manner. His partially gilded helmet has a large scale-covered aventail; there is also a flap of mail protecting the front of his throat. The internal scales of his cuirass are secured by small rivets, the visible heads of which are gilded. His leg defences are mail beneath gilded steel poleyns. On his left hip are a *jamdhar* and two swords, a normal sabre and a particularly long straight-bladed weapon. The horse's head-protecting chamfron again consists of a highly decorated fabric-covered bronze frame with a bar rising between the animal's ears. (Main sources: *Ghengiz Khan Nama*, Mughul manuscript c.1596, Nat. Lib., Tehran; *Hamza Nama*, Mughul manuscript c.1562–77, Seattle Art Museum, inv. 68.160, Seattle; *Akbar Nama*, Mughul manuscript, c.1590, Victoria & Albert Mus., inv. IS 201896, London.)

C2: Tabinan (cavalry trooper)

The equipment of this ordinary trooper is basically the same as his *mansabdar* officer. Beneath a light woollen tunic he has an early form of mail-and-plate cuirass while his legs are partially covered with scale-lined armour. His tapering form of *khanda* sword now has a knuckle-guard beneath its large

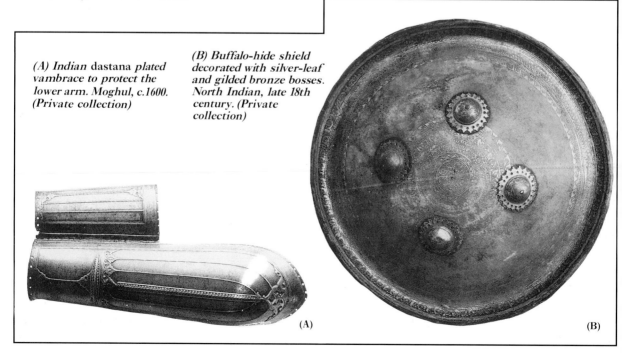

(A) Indian *dastana* plated vambrace to protect the lower arm. Moghul, c.1600. (Private collection)

(B) Buffalo-hide shield decorated with silver-leaf and gilded bronze bosses. North Indian, late 18th century. (Private collection)

(A)

(B)

disc-shaped pommel. Note that his spiral-cane shield has a cotton fringe around its boss, a fashion seen in late Mamluk Egypt and early Ottoman Turkey. The hat-like object on the horse's head may be a rudimentary chamfron. (Main sources: *Akbar Nama*, Mughul manuscript, c.1590, Victoria & Albert Mus., inv. IS 201896, London; *Babur Nama*, Mughul manuscript c.1598, Nat. Mus., Ms. 50.326, New Delhi; *Ghengiz Khan Nama*, Mughul manuscript c.1596, Nat. Lib., Tehran.)

C3: Barawardi light cavalry leader from Afghanistan

The only armour worn by this tribal warrior is a mail-lined fabric-covered *kazaghand*, more typical of Iran and the Middle East than of India. Otherwise he wears Turkish-influenced Afghan costume, and is armed with a simple sabre, a Persian dagger and a large leather-covered shield. (Main sources: *Anwar-i Sulayh*, Mughul manuscript c.1570, SOAS, London; *Akbar Nama*, Mughul manuscript, c.1590, Victoria & Albert Mus., inv. IS 201896, London; *Babur Nama*, Mughul manuscript c.1598, Nat. Mus., Ms. 50.326, New Delhi.)

D: Akbar's infantry & artillery, late 16th–early 17th centuries

Artillery was an important part of Akbar's armies and was relatively effective but not very mobile. The main functions of the infantry were to hold fixed positions, defend the artillery and to leave most manoeuvre to the cavalry.

D1: Infantry officer

Some foot soldiers appear quite finely dressed in Mughul art, and are probably officers. This man's long coat is tied with six pairs of bright laces down the right side and his sash is of the finest Kashmir wool. In addition to his archery equipment he also carries a large *nachakh* infantry axe and has a particularly fine ivory-hilted dagger on a narrow silk belt. (Main sources: *Babur Nama*, Mughul manuscript, c.1598, Musée Guimet, Paris; *Hamza Nama*, Mughul manuscript c.1562–77, Museum für angewandte Kunst, Vienna; *Hamza Nama*, Mughul manuscript c.1562–77, Seattle Art Museum, inv. 68.160.)

'Maharao Ram Singh I of Kota hunting rhinoceros on an elephant', Rajput painting c.1690. This fragmentary illustration shows how riders remained on the back of an elephant, the man at the front tucking his feet inside the animal's collar while the man at the back tucks his knees under a rope which runs beneath the elephant's tail. (Private collection)

D2: Artilleryman

The way this man has wound his turban shows him to be of Indian origin. His jacket with its cut-away front also only appears in Mughul art. In addition to a straight *khanda* sword on a baldric, a small shield hanging on his belt and a large curved dagger, he also carries a powder-horn and an iron 'touche' used to fire a cannon. (Main sources: *Khamsa of Nizami*, Mughul manuscript 1595, Brit. Lib., Ms. Or. 12208, London; *Hamza Nama*, Mughul manuscript c.1562–77, Museum für angewandte Kunst, Vienna.)

D3: Indian bumi (militiaman)

Mughul paintings portray Hindu Indian infantrymen dressed and equipped in a different manner to any other figures. This man has been given several such features, including a long necklace, a cloth tied around both arms, black threads above the elbows, and bells around waist and legs. He also carries an Indian straight sword with a tapering blade, a leather shield and a large, simple bow. The cannon which he guards is on a bullock-drawn cart used solely for transportation. (Main sources for figure:

Mughul miniature showing 'The execution of Shah Lodi', Shah-jahan Nama, 1656–7. Both horses are armoured; one of the men at top right wears a helmet with a very unusual visor across the upper part of his face; otherwise the men have typical late Mughul equipment mostly *consisting of mail plus a few plates. Two figures in the lower right corner seem to wear early forms of the chahar-aina 'four-plate' cuirass over their* mail. (Ms. P. 188, f.94v, The Royal Collection © 1993 Her Majesty the Queen)

Mughul painting by Sur Das, c.1605, location unknown; *Nata Ragini*, provincial manuscript c.1600, Brit. Mus., inv. 1973-9-17-05; main source for cannon; *Akbar Nama*, Mughul manuscript, c.1590, Victoria & Albert Mus., inv. IS 201896.)

E: Akbar's elephants, late 16th–early 17th centuries

The effectiveness of war elephants seems to have been far greater than most European observers give credit. Some of the most detailed descriptions of the Mughul army come from the pens of Jesuit missionaries, who were particularly impressed by the elephants.

E1: Senior commander with elephant

This figure wears a hat of unusual style, probably showing Central Asian influence. The characteristic Mughul double-breasted coat, fastened by pairs of brightly coloured laces on the right side, is also of Turco-Mongol origin. In addition to his magnificently decorated sabre and archery equipment he has a peculiar form of *piazi* Indian mace whose head is attached to the haft by a leather strap; and a hooked elephant goad with an ivory handle. Though the elephant is magnificently decorated its harness is basically the same as that of all riding elephants. (Main sources: *Akbar Nama*, Mughul manuscript, c.1590, Victoria & Albert Mus., inv. IS 201896, London; 'seated prince', Mughul miniature c.1620, location unknown; ivory-mounted elephant goad, 17th cent., Nat. Museum, New Delhi.)

E2: Fighting elephant

The *mahout* in charge of this elephant is armoured in the simple style also favoured by Mughul cavalrymen. What appears to be a flap of mail strengthens the front of his mail-lined and quilted jacket; his legs are protected by flaps of bronze scale armour, but his feet are bare to help control the elephant. The gunner, of Ethiopian origin, is much more heavily armoured with an iron helmet, mail-and-laminate cuirass with quilted lining, bronze lames as well as the normal iron *dastana* vambraces, padded and probably mail-lined leg defences. When not in use his *gajnal* heavy musket rests in a wooden box on the elephant's back; here it is being fired to accustom the elephant to gunfire. The elephant

Mughul miniature showing 'Siege of the fort of Dharur', Shah-jahan Nama, 1656–7. The foot soldiers at the upper right are armed only with shields and swords, or a mace in the case of the officer. Several of the horsemen in the lower left corner still have mail-and-plate armour. But the most interesting feature is the matchlock musket, with its supporting fork, slung across one rider's back. (Ms. P. 188, f.92v, The Royal Collection © 1993 Her Majesty the Queen)

itself has no body-armour, but its ears, head and vulnerable trunk are protected by fabric-covered lamellar and mail. (Main sources: *Babur Nama*, Mughul manuscript c.1598, Nat. Mus., Ms. 50.326, New Delhi; 'Nur Jahan loading a musket', Mughul painting 1612–13, Raza Lib., inv. H.1021, Rampur.)

E3: Jesuit missionary

The figure is based on a Mughul source which shows a missionary wearing the normal costume of the Jesuit Order, plus a broad-brimmed hat against the Indian sun. His shoes, however, were clearly made locally. (Main source: 17th-century Mughul miniature, National Museum of India, New Delhi.)

F: The Age of Empire: mid- to late 17th century

Emperor Shah-jahan is shown here on a hunting trip, his musket supported on a folding bipod rather than the clumsy musket rest used in Europe at this time. The guardsmen F2 holds the Emperor's the trumpeter F3 holds his elaborately decorated horse.

F1: Emperor Shah-jahan

Mughul court costume was rich and elaborate, with the ruling élite wearing much jewellery; nevertheless it still consisted of a turban wound in the Indian manner and a long coat of essentially Turco-Mongol style. Naturally the Emperor has highly decorated *jamdhar* and curved *jambia* daggers. His matchlock musket is also inlaid with silver and mother-of-pearl. Shah-jahan's horse (held by F3) has comparably decorated harness and saddle, while its tail and legs are also stained with henna. (Main source: 'Shah-jahan', Mughul miniature 17th cent., Victoria & Albert Mus., London; 'Akbar hands his crown to Shah-jahan', *Minto Album*, Mughul painting 1631, Chester Beatty Library, Dublin; 'Jahangir suppressing a rebellion', Mughul painting c.1623, *Kevorkian Album*, Freer Gallery, Washington.)

F2: Imperial guardsman

During the second half of the 17th century Mughul arms and armour changed in many ways, most obviously with the appearance of large thickly padded collars worn on perhaps mail-lined coats.

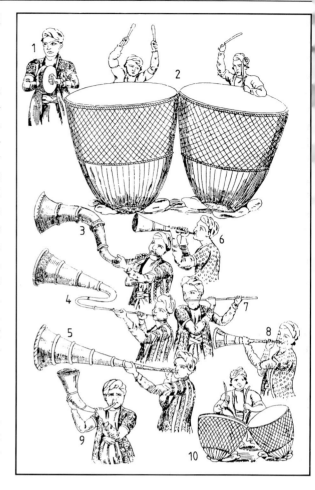

▲ *Mughul court and military musicians in a 19th-century engraving from an early 17th-century copy of the* Ain-i Akbari *manuscript: (1) sanj cymbals, (2) kuwargah large drums, (3–5) karana large horns, (6–7) surnas small horns, (8) nafir trumpet, (9) singh horn, (10) naqqarah small drums. (After Blochmann)*

◀ *Mughul miniature showing a 'wedding procession',* Shah-jahan Nama, *1656–7. A band playing assorted instruments and riding on elephants leads a group of officials carrying wedding presents. Note how the great drum is lashed to an elephant's back. (Ms. P. 188, f.122v, The Royal Collection © 1993 Her Majesty the Queen)*

Over such a coat this man wears an early type of *chahar-aina* four-plated cuirass. His helmet has a sliding nasal, and ear-flaps shown here raised. His own sabre is of the curved Indian *talwar* type whereas the Emperor's sword, which this guardsman carries in a silk bag, is of the straight *khanda* form. Horse-armour was now rarer and consists of a large flap-like piece over the animal's body plus a head-piece of complex construction. (Main source: *Padshah Nama*, Mughul manuscript 1640–45, Mus. Guimet, Paris; *Shahjehan Nama*, Mughul manuscript 1656, Royal Collection, Windsor; helmet, Mughul early 17th cent., Mus. für Völkerkunde, Vienna; 'Prince with advisors', Mughul painting by Bischr mid-17th cent, Chester Beatty Lib., Dublin; war-axe, Mughul 1650–1700, Armeria Reale, Turin.)

F3: Court trumpeter
Broadly striped coats appear in scenes of court life, though generally worn by low-ranking figures. Apart from his large double-curved *karana* trumpet he only has a curved *khanjar* dagger. (Main source: *Shahjehan Nama*, Mughul manuscript 1656, Royal Coll., Windsor; 'Akbar hands his crown to Shahjahan', *Minto Album*, Mughul painting 1631, Chester Beatty Lib., Dublin.)

G: Court life, late 17th–early 18th centuries
Much of Mughul court life took place out of doors or in tented enclosures. It remained as splendid as ever even as Mughul power declined. The horseman from Hyderabad appears to be bringing bad news.

G1: Mughul prince
The use of semi-transparent gauze fabric made sense in the Indian climate; it is interesting to note that it was also seen in the late 17th and early 18th-century Ottoman Court far to the west. In addition to his other highly decorated weaponry this prince

has an all-steel bow (held by G3). Such weapons were developed in India, where they resisted the hot, humid climate better than composite bows; they did not, however, have better performance. (Main sources: 'Shah-jahan', Mughul miniature 17th cent., Victoria & Albert Mus., London; 'Jahangir suppresses a rebellion', *Kevorkian Album*, Mughul miniature c.1623, Freer Gall., Washington; Court coat of a Mughul ruler, 1600–1650, Victoria & Albert Mus., London.)

G2: Heavy cavalryman from Hyderabad
Very heavily armoured cavalry came back into fashion in the autonomous Mughul province of Hyderabad in the 18th century. This man has a flexible mail-and-plate helmet worn over a thickly padded cap, a form of defence that went back almost 2,000 years in India. His long mail hauberk has chest and abdomen plates attached to the outer surface, the mail itself consisting of mixed *ganga-jamni* iron and gilded links; this name refers to the mixing of the clear waters of the Jumna River with the muddy waters of the Ganges. His shield is of steel. His *talwar* sword has a falchion-style blade while his *tabarzin* axe would be kept in a partially gilded leather case. (Main source: 'Sultan Shuja at the battle of Bahadarpur', Mughul miniature c.1658, private coll.; armour & helmet, northern

Mughul miniature showing 'Mughuls taking Hooghly from the Portuguese', Shah-jahan Nama, 1656–7. A line of ships, one end of which is tied to the shore, bombard the Portuguese fleet. Light cannon are mounted in their bows while various members of the crew shoot with matchlocks or bows. (Ms. P. 188, f.117r The Royal Collection © 1993 Her Majesty the Queen)

Another part of the Mughul miniature of the Mughuls taking Hooghly from the Portuguese, *Shah-jahan Nama, 1656–7,* shows a shore battery of heavier cannon shooting at the enemy fleet. (Ms. P. 188, f.117r The Royal Collection © 1993 Her Majesty the Queen)

India 17–18th cents., Royal Armouries, Tower of London; leg & foot armour, Mughul early 18th cent., Nat. Mus., New Delhi; dagger, Mughul c.1750, Nat. Mus., New Delhi; '*Khanda* of Aurangzeb', Mughul sword late 17th cent., Nat. Mus., New Delhi; war-axe, Mughul early 18th cent., Castle Museum, Powys, Wales.)

G3: Mughul court lady

Mughul female court costume was less elaborate than that of the men but could still be magnificent. The tall jewel-studded hat might have been reserved for ladies of rank. The rest of her dress is based on Indian rather than Muslim fashions and was designed for the hot Indian climate. (Main sources: fabric wall hanging, Madras region c.1640–50, Met. Mus. of Art, inv. 20.79, New York.)

H: Fall of the Mughuls, early to mid-18th century

An attack on a Mughul fortress by some of the Mughuls' Hindu enemies, the Rajputs and the Marathas. It is said that the Marathas trained monitors or large lizards to climb the walls of Mughul fortresses with ropes tied around their bodies; they then lodged themselves in crevices so that attackers could climb the rope!

H1: Rajput Zamindar

Certain aspects of costume characterised the 18th-century Hindu Rajput military élite, most obviously coats with very full lower skirts. This Hindu cavalry leader wears another form of mail-and-plate helmet with face-covering mail aventail, and a *chahar-aina* cuirass supported by shoulder straps strengthened with strips of mail. On his left hip he has a *khanda*

'Raja Jaswant Singh of Jodhpur with courtiers', Rajput drawing, c.1645. The weapons and costume of the Hindu Rajputs differed only in minor details from those of the ruling Muslim Mughuls by the mid-17th century. One of the few distinctions was that Rajput officers were frequently shown with their coats fastened on the left side of the body whereas Mughul officers had theirs fastened on the right. (Victoria & Albert Mus., inv. IS.559–1952)

a 'fencing-bar' which served as a rudimentary buckler. (Main sources: 'Sivaji on the march', Maratha manuscript early 18th cent., Bib. Nat., Paris; Maratha helmets 18th cent., Hermitage Museum, St. Petersburg & ex-Egerton of Tatton Coll., present location unknown; *peti* cuirass, southern India 18th cent., Victoria & Albert Mus., London; gauntlet-sword, India 18th cent., Museo Stibbert, Florence; fencing-bar, Maratha 18th cent., ex-Egerton of Tatton Coll., present location unknown.)

H3: Maratha nayak (infantry NCO)
This infantryman wears his coat laced down the left side in the Hindu fashion, and has daubed his face with turmeric to symbolise his willingness to die. His weapons include an extravagantly curved *bank* dagger and an all-steel 'gauntlet-mace'. (Main sources: 'Rana Amar Singh II of Mewar', Rajput painting c.1700, private collection.)

Rajput warrior in a 19th-century engraving from an 18th-century Rajput painting. (After Pant)

sabre and the reverse-curved *sosun patta* sword popular in southern India. He also carries a *jaghnol* 'dagger-bladed' war-axe. (Main sources: *jaghnol* war-axe, Rajastani c.1725, Nat. Mus. New Delhi; helmet, northern India 17–18th cents., Royal Armouries, Tower of London; 'Maharaja Kesari Singh fighting a lion', Rajput painting, 1715–20, Lallgarh Palace, Bikaner; Rajput sabre, late 17th cent., Nat. Mus., New Delhi; *sosun patta* sword, India 1770, Wallace Collection, inv. 2238, London.)

H2: Maratha poligar (light cavalryman)
Some extraordinary arms and armour appeared in southern India, developed from weapons known for over a thousand years. This warrior's helmet is of a typically Maratha shape, while his *peti* cuirass is made of numerous layers of cotton cloth. His weapons consist of a *patta* gauntlet-sword held by a horizontal grip like that of the *jamdhar* dagger, and

GLOSSARY

Ahadi: élite cavalryman not yet allocated *mansab* officer rank.

Bakhshi: Mughul military paymaster.

Bumi: auxiliary levy, mostly Hindu and mostly infantry.

Dakhili: Mughul professional soldier, paid directly by the state.

Diwan: senior financial controller of large province, late 17th–18th centuries (from Arabic *diwan*, government ministry).

Fauj: district; hence **Faujdar**: district governor.

Ghatwal: local governor in small frontier district, 18th century.

Kotwal: urban police chief, 16th–17th century.

Mansab: Mughul officer rank; hence **Mansabdar**: holder of officer rank.

Marathas: Hindu people of south-west India, powerful in 17th–18th centuries.

Mir: senior officer, from Arabic *amir*.

Nama: book or story.

Nazim, Nizam: governor of large province, late 17th–18th centuries.

Nayak: lowest infantry NCO in Maratha army,

(A)

(B)

Late Mughul armour: (A) helmet, breast and back plate, arm-defences and iron shield from Hyderabad, 18th century; (B) helmet and mail-and-plate body armour, northern India, 17th–18th centuries. (Royal Armouries, Tower of London)

17th–18th centuries; later an NCO rank in the British Indian army.

Poligar: Maratha light cavalryman.

Rajputs: Hindu people of Western India.

Sawar: Mughul rank, indicating specific military obligation.

Suba: province; hence **Subadar**: provincial governor; later a junior commissioned rank in the British Indian army.

Tabin, Tabinan: ordinary Mughul cavalry trooper.

Timurid: dynasty founded by Timur-i-Lenk (Tamerlane).

Tuman: large cavalry unit, originally a Mongol term.

Yigit: 'brave', Turkish warrior 15th–16th centuries.

Zamindar: Hindu military leader, often in Mughul service.

FURTHER READING

Abdul Aziz, *The Mansabdari System and the Mughul Army* (Lahore 1945)

Abu'l Fazl 'Allami (trans. H. Blochmann), *The Ain-i-Akbari of Abu'l Fazl 'Allami* (Calcutta 1873)

Babur (transl. A.S. Beveridge), *The Babur-nama in English* (London 1921)

L. Binyon, *Akbar* (London 1932)

R. Burn & W. Haig (editors), *The Cambridge History of India, Vol. IV: The Mughul Period* (Cambridge 1937)

U.N. Day, *The Mughul Government AD 1556–1707* (New Delhi 1970)

Egerton of Tatton, Lord, *A Description of Indian and Oriental Armour* (London 1896)

Encyclopedia of Islam (2nd edition), (Leiden 1960 continuing); articles on: Akbar, Awrangzib, Babur, Barud: India, Burdj: the tower in Islamic architecture in India, Djahangir, Djat, Harb: India, Hind, Hisar: Humayun, Lashkar

V. Fass, *The Forts of India* (London 1986)

S.Z. Haidar, *Islamic Arms and Armour of Muslim India* (Lahore 1991)

W. Irvine, *The Army of the Indian Moghuls: its organization and administration* (London 1903)

Monserrate (J.S. Hoyland trans.), *The Commentary of Father Monserrate S.J. on his Journey to the Court of Akbar* (London 1922)

'Sultan Shuja at the battle of Bahadarpur', Mughul manuscript illustration, c.1658–60. This simple drawing shows the Mughul usurper who ruled Bengal for a short time with his officers, each in the relatively light equipment typical of the later Mughul period. (Private collection)

G.N. Pant, *Mughul Weapons in the Babur-Nama* (Delhi 1989)

G.N. Pant, *Studies in Indian Weapons and Warfare* (New Delhi 1970)

H.R. Robinson, *Oriental Armour* (London 1967)

J.N. Sarkar, *The Military Despatches of a Seventeenth Century Indian General* (Calcutta 1969)

S. Toy, *The Fortified Cities of India* (London 1965)

S. Toy, *The Strongholds of India* (London 1957)

Notes sur les planches en couleurs

A Cette planche illustre les premiers Mughuls qui traversent les montagnes de l'Asie Centrale jusqu'à l'Afghanistan et les Indes. **A1** Babur, le premier conquérant mughul, porte un costume turc semblable à celui porté au cours de l'époque de Tamerlane: le manteau en soie, le pantalon et les bottes sont richement décorés. **A2** Le brave bien armé porte l'armure de style Timurid; à noter le casque avec petite banderole, et ce qu'on appelle la 'cuirasse chinoise', formé de plusieurs plaques de fer de tailles différentes. Son cheval porte une armure en cuir renforcé avec de la toile, la protection à sa tête est en bronze recouvert de cuir. **A3** Ce fantassin dirige un chameau qui porte les bagages et il porte un turban léger et une peau de mouton. Il a un carquois pour ses flèches mais pas d'étui pour son arc.

B Les premières fois que les Mughuls ont essayé de conquérir les Indes, ils ont entraîné plusieurs batailles entre musulmans, et le conflit se transforme en 'guerre civile'. **B1** La couleur rouge – ici sur le turban – semble indiquer les troupes qui sont directement sous le contrôle de l'Empire. Il porte un étendard doré avec trois queues de yak. **B2** Les cavaliers d'élite des Indes du Nord portent une armure très décorative, et utilisent un équipement pour les chevaux avant même l'arrivée des Mughuls; à noter les plaques de bronze et les mailles de fer qui s'alternent. **B3** Habillé comme un paysan, il tire son mousquet derrière une barrière en bois.

C1 Officier de cavalerie habillé de toute splendeur – son armure consiste d'écailles dorées et de mailles. A noter l'utilisation de deux épées, une qui est droite, l'autre courbée. Il utilise aussi le bouclier rond en canne. **C2** Moins décoré que son officier, le cavalier porte une armure faite de mailles et de plaques sous sa tunique en laine. La tête du cheval est protégée par une armure rudimentaire. **C3** La seule armure ici est le 'kazaghan' du style iranien faite de mailles et de toile; l'habit est turc mais le style est d'influence afghane.

D L'artillerie joue un rôle assez important dans les armées Mughul mais on utilise l'infanterie plutôt dans des rôles statiques ou en tant que gardes. Pour sa transportation, on pose le canon sur une charrette tirée par des bœufs. **D1** Le manteau long et fin et l'écharpe à nœud en laine kashmir; hache d'infanterie 'nachakh' et arc. **D2** Turban de style musulman et veste mughul caractéristique. Il porte une corne à poudre et un baton de fer pour allumer un canon. **D3** A noter les caractéristiques du costume militaire hindou en comparaison avec le costume musulman: collier long, pièces en toile autour des deux bras, fils noirs au dessus des coudes, et les cloches aux jambes et à la taille.

E1 Les commandants Mughul montent à dos d'éléphants pour pouvoir surveiller une bataille par dessus les autres troupes. Ce commandant, ici il est descendu de l'éléphant, porte un chapeau et un manteau qui illustrent les influences de l'Asie Centrale; à noter aussi la massue à forme indienne avec sa tête attachée par une lanière; aiguillon pour éléphant. Harnais de l'éléphant est d'un style complèxe mais n'est pas différent des autres. **E2** Le 'mahout' (celui qui monte sur l'éléphant) porte une armure de cavalerie style simple mais il a les pieds nus pour mieux contrôler la bête. Le mousquetaire d'Ethiopie, qui est beaucoup mieux armé, tire son mousquet pour accoutumer l'éléphant aux coups de feu. La tête vulnérable de l'éléphant est protégée, ainsi que son tronc. **E3** Les meilleures descriptions des éléphants mughul sont faites par des missionnaires jésuites. Une source mughul illustre un Jésuite qui porte un chapeau à bord large pour lui protéger du soleil et des chaussures européennes.

F1 Malgré la richesse dans la décoration et les bijoux, même l'Empereur – ici à la chasse – porte l'habit régulier des Mughuls: le turban d'un style indien ainsi qu'un manteau qui s'attache sur le côté qui rappelle ses ancêtres mongols. **F2** Des changements dans l'armure effectés à fin du 17ème siècle comprennent des cols rembourrés sur les manteaux doublés de mailles, et la cuirasse 'chahar-aina' avec des plaques en quatre parties. Son sabre personnel est le 'talwar' indien courbé, mais il porte aussi le 'khanda' droit de l'Empereur dans un sac en soie. L'armure pour les chevaux devient de plus en plus rare. Le casque a un protège-nez à glissière ainsi qu'un protège-joues à charnière. **F3** Les manteaux à rayures larges sont portés par les fonctionnaires modestes appartennant à la cour. A noter que les jambes et la queue du cheval sont colorés avec du henné.

G1 La vie de cour des Mughul se passe en général en plein air; cette vie reste splendide, même quand le pouvoir Mughul baisse. **G1** Le tissue de gaze semi-transparent convient parfaitement au climat indien – il est utilisé aussi par les Ottomans. **G2** Une cavalerie très bien armée redevient à la mode à Hyderabad pendant cette époque, et on utilise les mélanges habituels d'écailles, de mailles et de plaques; le bouclier est en acier. **G3** L'habit de cour pour les femmes mughul est beaucoup moins élaboré que celui des hommes; souvent d'un style indien qui convient beaucoup mieux au climat que les styles musulmans.

H1 Manteau large caractéristique des Rajputs; autre modèle de casque en mailles et plaques; cuirasse 'chahar-aina'; 'khanda' droit et épée 'sosun patta' des Indes du Sud courbée à l'envers. **H2** Casque typique des Marathas, cuirasse en coton à couches, épée-gantelet et barre pour l'escrime. **H3** La fermeture sur le côté est caractéristique pour les manteaux hindous. Sa figure est barbouillée avec du curcuma signifiant qu'il sacrifiera sa vie au combat. Parmi les armes il y a un gantelet-massue. On dit que les Marathas entraînaient des lézards à escalader les murs des forteresses en emportant des cordes pour que les attaqueurs puissent y grimper.

Farbtafeln

A Diese Tafel zeigt die ersten Mogulen bei der Überquerung der Berge von Mittelasien nach Afghanistan und Indien. **A1** Der erste Eroberer der Mogulen, Babur, trägt turktatarische Kleidung, die sich kaum von der unterscheidet, die zur Zeit von Tamerlan üblich war: reich verzierte Seidenjacke, Hose und Stiefel. **A2** Schwer bewaffneter 'Krieger' mit Rüstung im Timurid-Stil; man beachte den Helm mit kleinem Wimpel, und den sogenannten 'chinesischen Küraß' aus Eisenblättchen verschiedener Größe. Sein Pferd trägt einen stoffbedeckten Schutz aus gehärtetem Leder mit einem Kopfstück aus lederüberzogener Bronze. **A3** Dieser Fußsoldat, der ein Lastkamel führt, trägt einen losen Turban und einen Schafsledermantel. Er hat einen Köcher für seine Pfeile aber keine Bogentasche bei sich.

B Bei den frühen Versuchen der Mogulen, Indien zu erobern, Kam es oft zu Kämpfen zwischen Moslem und Moslem, wodurch der Streit zu einer Art 'Bürgerkrieg' ausartete. **B1** Die Farbe rot – hier am Turban – kennzeichnete scheinbar Truppen, die direkt kaiserlichem Befehl unterstanden. Er trägt eine vergoldete Standarte mit drei Jakschwänzen. **B2** Die nordindische Elite-Kavallerie trug bereits vor dem Einfall der Mogulen reich verzierte Rüstungen und Pferdeausrüstungen; man beachte die versetzt angeordneten Bronzeplatten und den eisernen Kettenpanzer. **B3** Er ist im Grunde wie ein Bauer gekleidet, trägt einen Munitionsgürtel unter seiner Schärpe und feuert hinter einem hölernen Schutzschild hervor.

C1 Prachtvoll ausgerüsteter Kavallerie-Offizier; seine Rüstung besteht aus vergoldeten Schuppen und einem Panzerhemd. Man beachte die beiden Säbel: einer mit gerader Klinge und ein Krummsäbel, sowie den runden Rohrschild. **C2** Der Reiter trägt unter seinem wollenen Uniformrock einen Ketten- und Plattenküraß, der weniger verziert ist als der des Offiziers. Das Pferd hat einen primitiven Kopfschutz. **C3** Der Ketten- und Stoff-*Kazaghan* iranischen Stils ist seine einzige Rüstung; die Kleidung ist dem Stil nach afghanisch mit turktatarischem Einfluß.

D Die Artillerie spielte in der Mogulen-Armee eine relativ bedeutende Rolle, was bei der Infanterie weniger der Fall war, da sie hauptsächlich in statischer Funktion und als Artilleriewachen eingesetzt wurde. Die Kanone ruht auf einem Ochsenkarren, der lediglich zu Transportzwecken benutzt wurde. **D1** Man beachte den schönen, langen Mantel und die Schärpe aus Kaschmirwolle; die *Nachakh*-Infanterieaxt und den Bogen. **D2** Turban nach indischem Vorbild und charakteristische Mogulenjacke. Er hat ein Pulverhorn und ein Eisengerät, das zum Abschuß der Kanonen benutzt wurde. **D3** Man beachte die eher Hindu als moslemischen Unterscheidungsmerkmale der Militärbekleidung: lange Halskette, um beide Arme geknotete Stoffstreifen, schwarze Schnüre über den Ellbogen und Glöckchen an den Beinen und um die Taille.

E1 Die Befehlshaber der Mogulen ritten auf Elefanten, so daß sie den Schlachtverlauf über die Köpfe der anderen Truppen hinweg beobachten konnten. Dieser Kommandant, hier abgesessen, trägt einen Hut und Mantel mit mittelasiatischen Einflüssen; man beachte ebenso die indische Form des Streitkolbens, der am Kopf mit einem Riemen befestigt ist; sowie Elefantensporn. Das Elefantengeschirr entspricht, obgleich prächtig, dem Muster, das für alle Reitelefanten benutzt wurde. **E2** Der *Mahout* trägt eine einfache Rüstung im Kavallerie-Stil. Er ist barfuß, um den Kriegselefanten besser leiten zu können. Der äthiopische Schütze, der seine Muskete abfeuert, um den Elefanten an das Geschützfeuer zu gewöhnen, ist besser geschützt, wie auch der verletzbare Kopf und Rüssel des Elefanten. **E3** Einige der besten Beschreibungen von Mogulen-Elefanten stammen von Jesuiten-Missionaren. Eine mogulische Quelle zeigt einen Jesuiten mit breitkrempigem Sonnenhut und einheimischen Schuhen.

F1 Trotz der prächtigen Verzierungen und dem Schmuck trägt selbst der Kaiser – hier bei einem Jagdausflug – die mogulisch-indische Standardbekleidung: den Turban im indischen Stil mit einem seitwärts geknoteten Mantel, der an seine Mogulen-Vorfahren erinnert. **F2** Zu den Veränderugen, die Ende des 17. Jahrhunderts an den Rüstungen vorgenommen wurden, gehörten unter anderem die dick wattierten Kragen an kettengefütterten Mänteln und der vierteilige *Chahar-aina*-Plattenküraß. Bei seinem eigenen Säbel handelt es sich um den indischen *Talwar*-Krummsäbel, doch trägt er den geradklingigen *Khanda* des Kaiser in einer Seidenhülse. Pferdepanzer wurden seltener. Der Helm hat einen gleitenden Nasenschutz und klappbaren Backenschutz. **F3** Bilder zeigen niedrige Höflinge in breitgestreiften Mänteln. Man beachte die Hennafärbung an den Beinen und am Schwanz des Pferds des Kaisers.

G Das Leben am Hof der Mogulen spielte sich hauptsächlich im Freien ab; selbst als die Macht der Mogulen verblaßte, blieb es prachtvoll. **G1** Der halb durchsichtige Gazestoff erwies sich im heißen indischen Klima als vernünftig und wurde auch von den Ottomanen benutzt. **G2** In Hyderabad kam zu dieser Zeit wieder schwer gerüstete Kavallerie in Mode, bei der man die übliche Kombination von Schuppen-, Ketten- und Plattenpanzer benutzte; der Schild ist aus Stahl. **G3** Die Bekleidung für Mogulenfrauen am Hof war weniger aufwendig als die der Männer; sie tendierte eher zum indischen Stil, der für das Klima besser geeignet war als der moslemische war.

H1 Charakteristischer Rajput-Mantel mit weitem Rock; andere Form des Ketten- und Plattenhelms; *Chahar-aina-Küraß*; geradklingige *Khanda* und umgekehrt gebogene *Sosun patta*-Säbel aus Südindien. **H2** Typischer Maratha-Helm, gestufter Baumwollküraß; Panzerhandschuh-Schwert und Parrierstock zum Fechten. **H3** Die Linksseitige Schnürung kennzeichnete die Hindu-Mäntel. Sein Gesicht ist mit Gelbwurz eingerieben, was die Bereitschaft zum Tod symbolisiert. Zu den Waffen zählt ein Panzerhandschuh-Streitkolben. Man sagt den Marathas nach, sie hätten Waraneidechsen darauf abgerichtet, Festungsmauern hinaufzuklettern und Seile mitzunehmen, die die Angreifer dann hinaufklettern konnten . . .